BookLife PUBLISHING

©2023
BookLife Publishing Ltd.
King's Lynn, Norfolk
PE30 4LS, UK

All rights reserved.
Printed in China.

A catalogue record for this book is available from the British Library.

ISBN: 978-1-80505-015-5

Written by:
Charis Mather

Edited by:
Rebecca Phillips-Bartlett

Designed by:
Isabella Croker

FSC MIX Paper from responsible sources FSC® C113515

All facts, statistics, web addresses and URLs in this book were verified as valid and accurate at time of writing. No responsibility for any changes to external websites or references can be accepted by either the author or publisher.

AN INTRODUCTION TO BOOKLIFE RAPID READERS...

Packed full of gripping topics and twisted tales, BookLife Rapid Readers are perfect for older children looking to propel their reading up to top speed. With three levels based on our planet's fastest animals, children will be able to find the perfect point from which to accelerate their reading journey. From the spooky to the silly, these roaring reads will turn every child at every reading level into a prolific page-turner!

CHEETAH
The fastest animals on land, cheetahs will be taking their first strides as they race to top speed.

MARLIN
The fastest animals under water, marlins will be blasting through their journey.

FALCON
The fastest animals in the air, falcons will be flying at top speed as they tear through the skies.

Photo Credits
Images are courtesy of Shutterstock.com. With thanks to Getty Images, Thinkstock Photo and iStockphoto.
RECURRING – bansenn, RidiUmbrella. COVER – DirkVE, Stephen Coburn, Eric Gomez T, Nicoleta Ionescu, bansenn, RidiUmbrella, Venera_J. 4–5 – pathdoc, Anatoliy Karlyuk. 6–7 – Terrie L. Zeller, Pavel L Photo and Video. 8–9 – Photobac, Eric Gomez T. 10–11 – researcher97, haryigit, Paolo De Gasperis. 12–13 – StockSmartStart, Bowonpat Sakaew, New Africa. 14–15 – DirkVE, Richard Peterson, "ear trumpet 1" flickr photo by Eknath Gomphotherium https://flickr.com/photos/eknathgomphotherium/6006153874 shared under a Creative Commons (BY-NC) license. 16–17 – leungchopan, ilona.shorokhova. 18–19 – User-duck, Nigel M Openshaw, Magicleaf. 20–21 – Fredamas, Artorn Thongtukit. 22–23 – Olena Yakobchuk, NaMong Productions, PeopleImages.com – Yuri A.

CONTENTS

Page 4	Weird and Wonderful
Page 6	Umbrella Hats
Page 8	Belay Glasses
Page 10	Potato Power
Page 12	Sugar Glass
Page 14	Ear Trumpets
Page 16	Two-Way Mirror
Page 18	Broccoli
Page 20	Glass Armonica
Page 22	Interesting Inventions
Page 24	Glossary and Index

Words that look like <u>this</u> are explained in the glossary on page 24.

WEIRD and WONDERFUL

Humans are always coming up with creative ways to fix problems.

Sometimes, this means coming up with out-of-the-box inventions.

Some inventions are useful. Some are fun.

Other inventions are just plain weird!

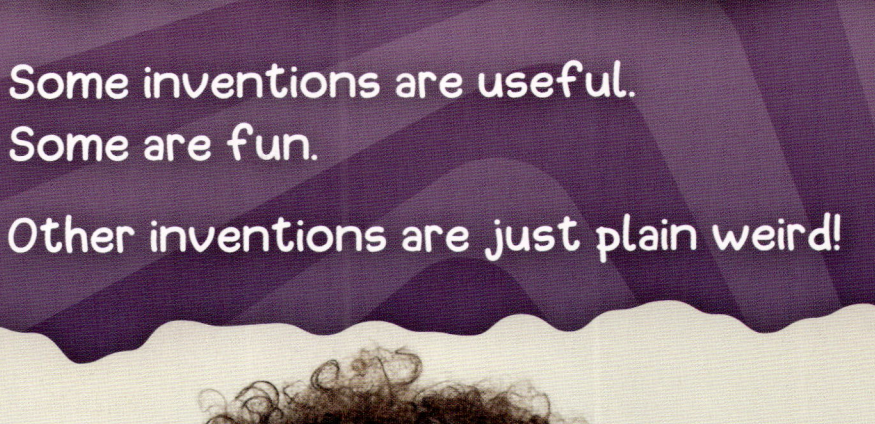

UMBRELLA HATS

Is carrying a normal umbrella in the rain too boring for you?

You could use an umbrella hat.

Umbrella hats help people keep their hands free while they are out in the rain.

BELAY GLASSES

People who hold the ropes for climbers are called belayers. They look up a lot, which can hurt their necks.

Some belayers use belay glasses to help them. These glasses let belayers see above them without looking up.

POTATO POWER

Did you know that potatoes can be batteries?

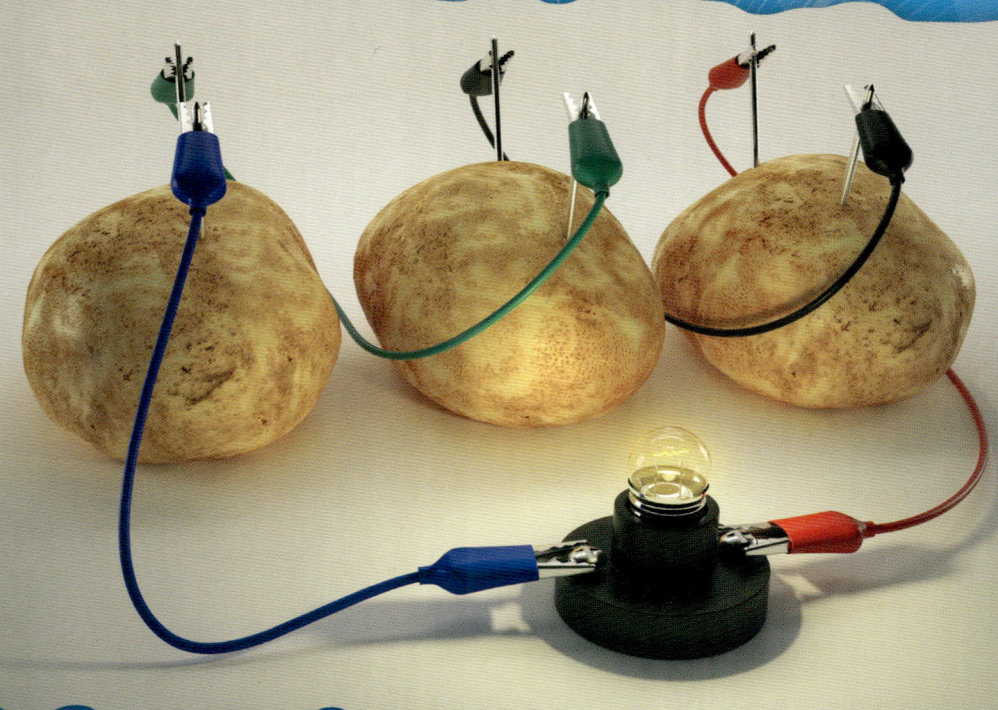

Potatoes are not <u>electric</u>, but electricity can pass through them.

If you plug the right metals into potatoes, you can power a small light!

Connecting more potatoes gives more power.

SUGAR GLASS

Sometimes, movie actors need to break <u>props</u>, such as glass bottles or windows. However, broken glass is very dangerous.

Actors may use sugar glass props instead.

Sugar glass looks just like real glass but is not as dangerous.

EAR TRUMPETS

If you lived about 200 years ago and could not hear very well, you might have used an ear trumpet.

Ear trumpets are not instruments that make music. They make other noises louder.

Ear trumpets came in many different shapes.

TWO-WAY MIRROR

From one side, two-way mirrors look just like normal mirrors.

Looking at this side only shows your reflection.

However, from the other side, two-way mirrors are see-through. They look like normal windows.

BROCCOLI

Did you know that broccoli did not always exist? This vegetable started as wild cabbage.

Wild cabbage

Over many years, people have <u>bred</u> wild cabbage flowers to taste better and better.

We now call this vegetable broccoli.

GLASS ARMONICA

Have you ever tried to play music with a glass?

The glass armonica takes this to the next level.

20

This instrument has lots of turning glass bowls. To play it, you wet your fingers and touch the bowls.

INTERESTING INVENTIONS

Have you got any interesting invention ideas?

No matter how weird they are, do not worry. There are probably weirder ideas out there.

Why not give being an inventor a go?

Who knows? Your invention might be the next big thing!

GLOSSARY

bred   caused to reproduce in a way that affects the characteristics of the offspring

electric   powered by electricity

props   objects used in a play or movie

reflection   the exact mirrored image of something

INDEX

batteries 10

ears 14–15

flowers 19

glass 8–9, 12–13, 20–21

instruments 15, 21

mirrors 16–17

potatoes 10–11